Dad

So day to day we forget about other people, especially those we love most - our family. This book is from me to you to let you know you are never forgotten

Sherry

Dear Father

Dear Father

Warm and Witty Writings About Fathers

Selected by Dean Walley

Illustrated by Muriel Wood

♛ HALLMARK EDITIONS

Dear Father

A Truly Giving Man

In her book Family Gathering, *novelist Kathleen Norris recalls her growing-up years near San Francisco. Here Miss Norris describes her father's gentle disposition:*

My father was the sole support of five unusually healthy and hungry children, his frail and clinging little sister Kitty, his wife with her fixed ideas of "niceness," which included fresh tablecloths daily, butter made into balls, children's underlinen changed three times weekly, and, of course, a cook in the kitchen and a young girl to help with beds, child care, and the Monday wash.

Added to these responsibilities was some regular and some emergency help for my mother's family, and the usual suburban outlay for commuter's tickets, carfare, club, lunches, and so on. He bought a surrey and an old horse named Hatrack; he bought a cow my mother really loved, Dolly; he bought an incubator for my brother Joe to manage so that we might always have chicken for Sunday lunch. Just how this was done on the salary paid the manager of a small private bank it is hard to understand now, but he did it, and was always optimistic, content, and ready with Sunday plans for long walks and picnics in Muir Woods over the hill some four miles away. We were always aware of his presence when he was in the house or anywhere about, for his interest in a thousand small things was vigorous and he usually wanted to share it with one of us.

He would read me a passage from Byron or Macaulay, under his green light in the study that was merely an alcove off the big homey sitting room, or he would call Teresa from her absorption in Gayley's *Classic Myths* to come and tell her poor old father that she loved him. Often when my mother finished some brilliant piano performance he would murmur, "Thanks, Jo. Wonderful!" without stopping his reading. Both older sons crossed the Bay with him on their way to school in San Francisco every morning, and as for the smaller children, they built block houses and walked chessmen about his feet, under his table, unrebuked.

Phrases of my father's making have lived long after him. Once, when in the discontented teens I was bewailing the fact, with that faculty all teenagers have for boring their hearers insufferably, that I was not as good-looking as my sister, mother, or aunts, my father said staunchly, "Well, even if it's so, we can't all be handsome. But I've always felt that a handsome man has only a twenty-minute start on me!" I've remembered this at many a dinner table when a Hollywood beauty happened to be at my host's left.

At another time some members of the home circle accused me of exaggeration. "Let her alone!"

said Dad. "Any good story deserves a top hat and a stick!"

And in defense of home hospitalities he quoted his Irish grandfather: "No man was ever carried to the poorhouse on his dining room table!"

'He Doesn't Ware a Beard'

Mark Twain had a special love for his daughter Susy Clemens, who responded in turn with a biography of him, written when she was thirteen years old. Here Samuel Clemens reveals what it meant to him:

When Susy was thirteen and was a slender little maid with plaited tails of copper-tinged brown hair down her back and was perhaps the busiest bee in the household hive, by reason of the manifold studies, health exercises and recreations she had to attend to, she secretly and of her own motion and out of love added another task to her labors—the writing of a biography of me.... I have had no compliment, no praise, no tribute from any source that was so precious to me as this one was....

It [was] quite evident that several times, at breakfast and dinner, in those long-past days, I was posing for the biography. In fact, I clearly remember that I was doing that—and I also remember that Susy detected it. I remember saying a very smart thing, with a good deal of an air, at the breakfast table one morning and that Susy observed to her mother privately a little later that papa was doing that for the biography. . . .

The spelling is frequently desperate but it was Susy's and it shall stand. I love it and cannot profane it. To me it is gold. To correct it would alloy it, not refine it. . . .

In her biography, Susy describes her famous father's appearance and some of his peculiarities: It is papa I am writing about, and I shall have no trouble in not knowing what to say about him, as he is a *very* striking character.

Papa's appearance has been described many times, but very incorrectly. He has beautiful gray hair, not any too thick or any too long, but just right; a Roman nose, which greatly improves the beauty of his features; kind blue eyes and a small mustache. He has a wonderfully shaped head and profile. He has a very good figure—in short, he is an extrordinarily fine looking man. All his features are perfect, exept that he hasn't extraordinary teeth. His complexion is very fair, and he doesn't ware a beard. He is a very good man and a very funny one. He *has* got a temper, but we all of us have in this family. He is the loveliest man I ever saw or ever hope to see—and oh, so absentminded. . . .

Papa has a peculiar gait we like, it seems just to sute him, but most people do not; he always walks up and down the room while thinking and between each coarse at meals.

Her father comments on Susy's observation: **A** lady distantly related to us came to visit us once in those days. She came to stay a week but all our efforts to make her happy failed and we could not imagine why, and she got up her anchor and sailed the next morning. We did much guessing but could not solve the mystery. Later we found out what the trouble was. It was my tramping up and down between courses. She conceived the idea that I could not stand her society.

Susy turns out to be an unprejudiced biographer: Papa uses very strong language, but I have an idea not nearly so strong as when he first married mamma. A lady acquaintance of his is rather apt to interupt what one is saying, and papa told mamma that he thought he should say to the lady's husband "I am glad your wife wasn't present when the Deity said Let there be light."

Sam Clemens appreciates his daughter's honesty: This is a frank historian. She doesn't cover up one's deficiencies but gives them an equal showing with one's handsomer qualities. Of course I made the remark which she has quoted—and even at this distant day I am still as much as half persuaded that if that lady mentioned had been present when the Creator said, "Let there be light" she would have interrupted him and we shouldn't ever have got it.

Susy comments on her father's lack of scholastic enterprise: And we know papa played "Hookey" all the time. And how readily would papa pretend to be dying so as not to have to go to school!

Sam Clemens draws a deduction from his daughter's perception: These revelations and exposures are searching but they are just. If I am as transparent to other people as I was to Susy I have wasted much effort in this life.

Susy evaluates her father's abilities: Grandma couldn't make papa go to school, so she let him go into a printing office to learn the trade. He did so, and gradually picked up enough education to enable him to do about as well as those who were more studious in early life.

Sam Clemens gives his daughter credit as a biographer: It is noticeable that Susy does not get overheated when she is complimenting me but maintains a proper judicial and biographical calm. It is noticeable also and it is to her credit as a biographer that she distributes compliment and criticism with a fair and even hand.

'A New Deal for Dad' Adlai Stevenson was not only an eminent statesman, but also a loving father. Here in an address before the National Father's Day Committee in 1961, he laments the lack of respect for fathers in contemporary times:

I have come here today not so much to accept an award as to strike a much-needed blow for father-hood in America.

There was a time when father amounted to something in the United States. He was held with some esteem in the community; he had some authority in his own household; his views were sometimes taken seriously by his children; and even his wife paid heed to him from time to time.

In recent years, however, especially since World War II, father has come upon sorry times. He is the butt of the comic strips; he is the boob of the radio and TV serials; and the favorite stooge of all our professional comedians.

In short, life with father seems to have degenerated into a continuous sequence of disrespect or tolerance at best. It appears that the poor fellow is unable to hang a picture or hit a nail without some mishap; no radio or lock will ever work again after he fixes it; he can't boil water or even barbecue a steak, at least not without burning it.

Every time the so-called head of the household attempts to assert himself or express his opinions, the whole family is convulsed with indulgent if not scornful laughter.

Personally, I think all this has gone far enough, and father certainly needs his Day! So all of us fathers should be grateful to you for contriving this brief hour of recognition. I am honored that you have chosen me, a father and a grandfather.

I do not think we would want father restored to his nineteenth century role of absolute monarch, but, even though we don't want him to be the autocrat of the breakfast table, I think we might consider giving him at least a polite seat at the table.

After forty or fifty years of life, after hard experience in the world of affairs, after education both in college and in the school of hard knocks, and after sweating away at earning a living for the whole family, it is conceivable that father could have learned a thing or two, and the rest of the family could listen to him with profit once in a while for the honor of raising a plaintive voice on behalf of so many. We might even have some better-behaved children if they did listen to him now and then. But of course I except my own children. I have to—or I might not survive Father's Day!

In all candor I cannot say that I know for sure just how seriously my own children listen to me, but, God bless them, they at least pretend they do.

So all things considered, I have this suggestion to offer: Instead of a Father's Day, maybe we should try a Father's Year for a change. In any case, whatever we call it, let's have a New Deal for Dad!

A Father for the Homeless

Father Flanagan of Boys Town was the very embodiment of fatherhood. His love and care for hundreds of foundlings began when the Omaha juvenile court awarded him custody of five homeless boys. It was December 12, 1917, that his first charges arrived in the ramshackle house where Boys Town started:

In the entrance hall the first two boys who arrived looked around with incredulous eyes, and the older one remarked: "We're sure gonna be living in a swell dump!"

Swell it did seem to their unaccustomed eyes. Alas, it was, in fact, no gleaming mansion. [Father Flanagan] had only a few weeks to gather the furnishings. . . . The result was a weird conglomeration of attic castoffs. . . .

A few nights after the home opened [Father Flanagan] woke up to hear one of the boys crying. He got up and stalked into the room to find the boy sitting up in bed. He had an earache. Now that was something new to Father Flanagan. What ought he to do? Call in a doctor?

"When I used to have an earache," another boy volunteered in a matter-of-fact tone, "my mother always used to hoist me up and carry me around and sing."

The priest in his nightgown pondered the problem dolefully. Then he lifted up the boy and began to pace up and down the room, humming a tune softly, from old memories of his mother and her "lulla-lullay" in Roscommon [Ireland]. In a little while the child was asleep, and Flanagan felt immensely proud of the therapuetic qualities of his voice....

Not any of these first five boys had committed crimes. Their worst offense lay in having no homes. The two who had been turned over to him by the juvenile court that morning were brothers. Many years later, during the second World War, one of these brothers wrote back to Father Flanagan from the Southwest Pacific:

"That morning in December of 1917 is indelibly stamped into my brain. I can never forget how, after the juvenile authorities had relinquished my brother and I and we were in your custody, you presented me with a bag of chocolates...."

FULTON AND WILL OURSLER

Many years I lost happiness. I sought it in knowledge, and found disillusionment. I sought it in writing, and found a weariness of the flesh. I sought it in travel, and my feet tired on the way. I sought it in wealth, and I found discord and worriment.

And then one day, at a little station out on a wooded cliff near the sea, I saw a woman waiting in a tiny car, with a child asleep in her arms. A man alighted from a train, walked to her quickly, embraced her, and kissed the child gently, careful lest he should awaken it. They drove off together to some modest home among the fields, and it seemed to me that happiness was with them.

Today I have neglected my writing. The voice of a little girl calling to me, "Come out and play," drew me from my papers and my books. Was it not the final purpose of my toil that I should be free to frolic with her, and spend unharrassed hours with the one who had given her to me? And so we walked and ran and laughed together, and fell in the tall grass, and hid among the trees; and I was young again.

Now it is evening; while I write, I hear the child's breathing as she sleeps in her cozy bed. And I know that I have found what I sought. I perceived that if I will do as well as I can the tasks for which life has made me, I shall find fulfillment, and a quiet lane of happiness for many years. Gladly I surrender myself to nature's imperative of love and parentage, trusting to her ancient wisdom.

> My father could not make a poem,
> But setting his course by yonder pine,
> Straight and true he plowed a line
> Across the field. My father could not
> Juggle words, but with the birth
> Of golden wheat in summer sun,
> He coaxed a poem out of the earth.
>
> MARY FERRELL DICKINSON

Last night my child was born—a very strong boy with large black eyes . . . If you ever become a father, I think the strangest and strongest sensation of your life will be hearing for the first time the thin cry of your own child. For a moment you have the strange feeling of being double; but there is something more, quite impossible to analyze— perhaps the echo in a man's heart of all the sensations felt by all the fathers and mothers of his race at a similar instant in the past. It is a very tender, but also a very ghostly feeling. LAFCADIO HEARN

Fanfare For Father

Fathers are exceptional creatures
Who inhabit armchairs and
    hammocks and bleachers.
Never placid or acid or humdrum,
It's the male of the species they come from.
That is to say they're of the masculine gender—
The sex which denies that its nature is tender.
Fathers are a credit to all Homo sapiens—
Indians, Spaniards, Germans and Lappians.
They hail from such places as Portland and Macon
And work very hard to bring home the bacon.
You can tell that they're different from mammas
By the size of their hats and pajamas.
They're tougher and stricter and stronger
And the reach of their arms is much longer.
These grown-up Tom Swifts and Tom Sawyers
Make excellent doctors and lawyers,
Tailors and sailors, whalers and draftsmen,
Salesmen, accountants and all kinds of craftsmen.
All fathers have whiskers and some have mustaches.
Theirs are the pockets where all the loose cash is.
Theirs are the heads where most of the brains are.
Theirs are the backs where most of the pains are.
No one is better at fractions and numbers.
No one is sadder at waltzes and rhumbas.

They're handy with hammers, chisels and pliers,
Bevels and levels and barbecue fires.
A father's the whole family's hero—
Part Lindbergh, part Tarzan, part Nero.
He has, it is clear, the patience of Job
And he's happiest wearing his slippers and robe.
As head of the house, he foots the bills
For chops and tops and coated pills,
For lamps and stamps and towels and sheets
And hats and bats and parakeets.
Give him a gift—say, a pipe or a belt—
And right on the spot a father will melt.
He'll listen in silence to most people's views,
But he'll argue like mad at the six o'clock news.
Fathers are sometimes extremely outspoken,
Especially on days when they're rudely awoken,
But soon as they see that chip off the block
They're inclined to forget the hands of the clock.
Though they can't ever find their sox or their specs,
Fathers are really a marvelous sex,
Happy-go-lucky, thoughtful of others,
The very best thing to be married to mothers.

LEONARD DOWTY

Help from Dad

I have now but one anxiety left,

which is, concerning you.

I would have you be,

what I know nobody is, perfect.

As that is impossible,

I would have you as near perfection

as possible.

LORD CHESTERFIELD

Mutual Concessions   *Alabama-born novelist Harper Lee won the Pulitzer Prize in 1961 with her book* To Kill a Mockingbird, *a story of a father and his young daughter in a Southern town. Here Atticus, the father, makes a compromise with his daughter, Scout, bringing a "day of misfortunes" to a happy and meaningful conclusion:*

After supper, Atticus sat down with the paper and called, "Scout, ready to read?" The Lord sent me more than I could bear, and I went to the front porch. Atticus followed me.

"Something wrong, Scout?"

I told Atticus I didn't feel very well and I didn't think I'd go to school any more if it was all right with him.

Atticus sat down in the swing and crossed his legs. His fingers wandered to his watchpocket; he said that was the only way he could think. He waited in amiable silence, and I sought to reinforce my position: "You never went to school and you do all right, so I'll just stay home too. You can teach me like Granddaddy taught you 'n' Uncle Jack.

"No I can't," said Atticus. "I have to make a living. Besides, they'd put me in jail if I kept you at home—dose of magnesia for you tonight and school tomorrow."

"I'm feeling all right, really."

"Thought so. Now what's the matter?"

Bit by bit, I told him the day's misfortunes. "—and she said you taught me all wrong, so we can't ever read any more, ever. Please don't send me back, please sir."

Atticus stood up and walked to the end of the porch. When he completed his examination of the wisteria vine he strolled back to me.

"First of all," he said, "if you can learn a simple trick, Scout, you'll get along a lot better with all kinds of folks. You never really understand a person until you consider things from his point of view—"

"Sir?"

"—until you climb into his skin and walk around in it."

Atticus said I had learned many things today, and Miss Caroline [the teacher] had learned several things herself. . . . We could not expect her to learn all Maycomb's ways in one day, and we could not hold her responsible when she knew no better.

"I'll be dogged," I said. "I didn't know no better than not to read to her, and she held me responsible—listen Atticus, I don't have to go to school!" I was bursting with a sudden thought. "Burris Ewell, remember? He just goes to school the first day. The truant lady reckons she's carried out the law when she gets his name on the roll—". . .

"You, Miss Scout Finch, are of the common folk. You must obey the law." He said that the Ewells were members of an exclusive society made up of Ewells. In certain circumstances the common folk judiciously allowed them certain privileges by the simple method of becoming blind to some of the Ewells' activities. They didn't have to go to school, for one thing. Another thing, Mr. Bob Ewell, Burris's father, was permitted to hunt and trap out of season.

"Atticus, that's bad," I said. In Maycomb County, hunting out of season was a misdemeanor at law, a capital felony in the eyes of the populace.

"It's against the law, all right," said my father, "and it's certainly bad, but when a man spends his relief checks on green whiskey his children have a way of crying from hunger pains. I don't know of any landowner around here who begrudges those children any game their father can hit."

"Mr. Ewell shouldn't do that—"

"Of course he shouldn't but he'll never change his ways. Are you going to take out your disapproval on his children?"

"No sir," I murmured, and made a final stand: "But if I keep on goin' to school, we can't ever read any more...."

"That's really bothering you, isn't it?"

"Yes sir."

When Atticus looked down at me I saw the expression on his face that always made me expect something. "Do you know what a compromise is?" he asked.

"Bending the law?"

"No, an agreement reached by mutual concessions. It works this way," he said. "If you'll concede the necessity of going to school, we'll go on reading every night just as we always have. Is it a bargain?"

"Yes sir!"

"We'll consider it sealed without the usual formality," Atticus said, when he saw me preparing to spit.

As I opened the front screen door Atticus said, "By the way, Scout, you'd better not say anything at school about our agreement."

"Why not?"

"I'm afraid our activities would be received with considerable disapprobation by the more learned authorities."

Jim and I were accustomed to our father's last-will-and-testament diction, and we were at all times free to interrupt Atticus for a translation when it was beyond our understanding.

"Huh, sir?"

"I never went to school," he said, "but I have a feeling that if you tell Miss Caroline we read every night she'll get after me, and I wouldn't want her after *me*."

Atticus kept us in fits that evening, gravely reading columns of print about a man who sat on a flagpole for no discernible reason, which was reason enough for Jim to spend Saturday aloft in the treehouse. . . .

For a person in rugged health who is not particularly dressed up and does not want to write a letter or read the newspaper, we can imagine few diversions more enjoyable than to have a child turned loose upon him.   HEYWOOD BROUN

'The Force of My Love'   *An eighteenth-century parliamentarian, Lord Chesterfield, wrote his son, Philip Stanhope, when Philip was abroad completing his education. The letters, which span a decade, are universal in their message: a father's love, a father's counsel, and a father's concern:*
Nineteen fathers in twenty, and every mother who had loved you half as well as I do, would have ruined you; whereas I always made you feel the weight of my authority, that you might one day know the force of my love. Now, I both hope and believe, my authority had from necessity [to be

applied]. My advice is just eight-and-thirty years older than your own, and consequently, I believe you think, rather better.

We must take things as they are, we cannot make them what we would, nor often what they should be.

Depend upon it, you will sink or rise to the level of the company which you commonly keep;— people will judge of you, and not unreasonably, by that. There is good sense in the Spanish saying, "Tell me whom you live with, and I will tell you who you are."

Men are more unwilling to have their weaknesses and their imperfections known, than their crimes; and, if you hint to a man that you think him silly, ignorant, or even ill-bred or awkward, he will hate you more and longer, than if you tell him plainly that you think him a rogue.

There are many companies which you will and ought to keep . . . your own good sense must distinguish the company and the time. You must trifle with triflers, and be serious only with the serious; but dance to those who pipe.

With nine people in ten, good-breeding passes for good-nature, and they take attentions for good offices.

Speak the language of the company that you are in; speak it purely, and unlarded with any other.

Never seem wiser, nor more learned, than the people you are with. Wear your learning, like your watch, in a private pocket; and do not pull it out and strike it merely to show you have one.

I have now but one anxiety left, which is, concerning you. I would have you be, what I know nobody is, perfect. As that is impossible, I would have you as near perfection as possible.

'Believe in Yourself' *American poet and father William Carlos Williams offers sympathetic advice to his son away at college:*

Dearest Bill:

This I can say for certain, you seem not far different from what I was myself at your age. . . . Everything seems upside down and one's self the very muck under one's foot.

It comes from many things, my dear boy, but mostly from the inevitable maladjustment consequent upon growing up in a more or less civilized environment. . . . But more immediately, your difficulties arise from a lack of balance in your daily life, a lack of balance which has to be understood and withstood—for it cannot be avoided for the present. I refer to the fact that your intellectual life, for the moment, has eclipsed the physical life, the animal life, the normal he-man life, which every man needs and craves. . . .

You, dear Bill, have a magnificent opportunity to enjoy life ahead of you. You have sensibility (even if it drives you nuts at times) which will be the source of keen pleasures later and the source of useful accomplishments too. You've got a brain, as you have been told *ad nauseum*. But these are things which are tormenting you, the very things which are your most valued possessions and which will be your joy tomorrow. Sure you are sentimental, sure you admire a man like Wordsworth and his "Tintern Abbey." It is natural, it is the correct reaction of your age to life. It is also a criticism of Wordsworth as you will see later. All I can say about that is, wait! Not wait cynically, idly, but wait while looking, believing, getting fooled, changing from day to day. Wait with the only kind of faith I have ever recognized, the faith that says I wanna know!

Meanwhile I'm not making any final judgments. Wait it out. Don't worry too much. You've got time. You're all right. You're reacting to life in the only way an intelligent, sensitive young man in college can. In another year, you'll enter another sphere of existence, the practical one. The knowledge, abstract now, which seems unrelated to sense to you (at times) will get a different color.

Sooner or later we all of us knock our heads against the ceiling of the world. It's like breaking a record: the last fifth of a second, which marks the difference between a good runner and a world beater is the hardest part of the whole proceeding. I mean that you, Bill, will be one of the minds of the world tomorrow. You will be the one, you and your generation, who will have to push knowledge of all sorts that inch ahead, which will make life tolerable in your day. Knowledge is limited, very limited, and it is only because you are in the pre-liminary stages of knowing that you think men, certain men, know so much more than you do. They may know more, but not the great amount that you imagine. For this reason, wait!

Believe in yourself and your generation. Take it with a smile. That's what they mean when they speak of humor. It doesn't mean a guffaw or a grin. It means steadiness of nerves that is willing to bide its time, certain that with time a human adjust-ment can and will be made. It is the most that any man has ever been able to do. . . .

Mother and I both send love. Don't let *anything* get your goat and don't think you have to duck anything in life. There is a way out for every man who has the intellectual fortitude to go on in the face of difficulties.

Yours, Dad

'To Thine Own Self Be True'

In William Shakespeare's play Hamlet, Polonius instructs his son Laertes in the prerequisites of manhood:

These few precepts in thy memory
See thou character. Give thy thoughts no tongue,
Nor any unproportion'd thought his act.
Be thou familiar, but by no means vulgar.
The friends thou hast, and their adoption tried,
Grapple them to thy soul with hoops of steel;
But do not dull thy palm with entertainment
Of each new-hatch'd, unfledg'd comrade. Beware
Of entrance to a quarrel: but being in,
Bear't that th' opposed may beware of thee.
Give every man thine ear, but few thy voice:
Take each man's censure, but reserve thy
  judgment.
Costly thy habit as thy purse can buy.
But not express'd in fancy: rich, not gaudy;
For the apparel oft proclaims the man.
Neither a borrower nor a lender be;
For loan oft loses both itself and friend,
And borrowing dulls the edge of husbandry.
This above all: to thine own self be true;
And it must follow, as the night the day,
Thou canst not then be false to any man.

No Name Of My Own

Life With Father, one of the best-loved books of American family humor, depicts the growing-up years of Clarence Day and his struggles in a patriarchal household. Here, he laments the problems of being a Junior:

Father and I would have had plenty of friction in any case. This identity of names made things worse. . . .

He opened everything that came addressed to Clarence S. Day, Jr. He didn't do this intentionally, but unless the "Jr." was clearly written, it looked like "Esq.," and anyhow Father was too accustomed to open all Clarence Day letters to remember about looking carefully every time for a "Jr." So far as mail and express went, I had no name at all of my own.

For the most part nobody wrote to me when I was a small boy except firms whose advertisements I had read in the *Youth's Companion* and to whom I had written requesting them to send me their circulars. These circulars described remarkable bargains in magicians' card outfits, stamps and coins, pocket knives, trick spiders, and imitation fried eggs, and they seemed interesting and valuable to me when I got them. The trouble was that Father usually got them and at once tore them up. I then had to write for such circulars again, and if Father got the second one too, he would sometimes explode with annoyance. He became particularly indignant one year, I remember, when he was repeatedly urged to take advantage of a special bargain sale of false whiskers. He said that he couldn't understand why these offerings kept pouring in. I knew why, in this case, but at other times I was often surprised myself at the number he got, not realizing that as a result of my postcard request my or our name had been automatically put on several large general mailing lists. . . .

After Father had stormily endured these afflictions for a while, he and I began to get letters from girls. Fortunately for our feelings, these were rare, but they were ordeals for both of us. Father had forgotten, if he ever knew, how silly young girls can sound, and I got my first lesson in how unsystematic they were. No matter how private and playful they meant their letters to be, they forgot to put "Jr." on the envelope every once in so often. When Father opened these letters, he read them all the way through, sometimes twice, muttering to himself over and over: "This is very peculiar. I don't understand this at all. Here's a letter to me from some person I never heard of. I can't see what it's about." By the time it had occurred to him that possibly the letter might be for me, I was red and embarrassed and even angrier at the girl than at father. And on days when he had read some of the phrases aloud to the family, it nearly killed me to claim it. . . .

In the days when Mrs. Pankhurst and her friends were chaining themselves to lampposts in London, in their campaign for the vote, a letter came from Frances Hand trustfully asking "Dear Clarence" to do something to help Woman Suffrage—speak at a meeting, I think. Father got red in the face. "Speak at one of their meetings!" he roared at Mother. "I'd like nothing better! You can tell Mrs. Hand that it would give me great pleasure to inform all those crackpots in petticoats exactly what I think of their antics."

"Now, Clare," Mother said, "you mustn't talk that way. I like that nice Mrs. Hand, and anyhow this letter must be for Clarence.". . .

Once in a while when I got a letter that I had no time to answer I used to address an envelope to the sender and then put anything in it that happened to be lying around on my desk—a circular about books, a piece of newspaper, an old laundry bill— anything at all, just to be amiable, and yet at the same time to save myself the trouble of writing. I happened to tell several people about this private habit of mine at a dinner one night—a dinner at which Alice Duer Miller and one or two other writers were present. A little later she wrote me a criticism of Henry James and ended by saying that

I needn't send her any of my old laundry bills because she wouldn't stand it. And she forgot to put on the "Jr."

"In the name of God," Father said bleakly, "this is the worst yet. Here's a woman who says I'd better not read *The Golden Bowl*, which I have no intention whatever of doing, and she also warns me for some unknown reason not to send her my laundry bills."

The good part of all these experiences, as I realize now, was that in the end they drew Father and me closer together. My brothers had only chance battles with him. I had a war. Neither he nor I relished its clashes, but they made us surprisingly intimate.

'All I Believe In' *American novelist F. Scott Fitzgerald not only captured the temper of the '20s in his books but he also captured the attentions of his little girl in his letters to her. The following is his prescription for living written when she was eleven years old:*

Dear Pie:
I feel very strongly about your doing [your] duty. Would you give me a little more documentation about your reading in French? I am glad you are

happy—but I never believe much in happiness. I never believe in misery either. Those are things you see on the stage or the screen or the printed page, they never really happen to you in life.

All I believe in in life is the rewards for virtue (according to your talents) and the *punishments* for not fulfilling your duties, which are doubly costly. If there is such a volume in the camp library, will you ask Mrs. Tyson to let you look up a sonnet of Shakespeare's in which the line occurs *Lilies that fester smell far worse than weeds.*

Have had no thoughts today, life seems composed of getting up a *Saturday Evening Post* story. I think of you, and always pleasantly; but if you call me "Pappy" again I am going to take the White Cat out and beat his bottom *hard, six times for every time you are impertinent.* Do you react to that?

I will arrange the camp bill. Half-wit, I will conclude.

Things to worry about: Worry about courage / Worry about cleanliness / Worry about efficiency / Worry about horsemanship . . . .

Things not to worry about: Don't worry about popular opinion / Don't worry about dolls / Don't worry about the past / Don't worry about the future / Don't worry about growing up / Don't worry about anybody getting ahead of you / Don't worry about triumph / Don't worry about failure unless it comes through your own fault/Don't worry about mosquitoes/Don't worry about flies/Don't worry about insects in general/Don't worry about parents/Don't worry about boys/Don't worry about disappointments/Don't worry about pleasures/Don't worry about satisfactions.

Things to think about: What am I really aiming at? How good am I in comparison to my contemporaries in regard to: (a) Scholarship (b) Do I really understand about people and am I able to get along with them? (c) Am I trying to make my body a useful instrument or am I neglecting it?

With dearest love,
Daddy

P.S. My come-back to your calling me Pappy is christening you by the word Egg, which implies that you belong to a very rudimentary state of life and that I could break you up and crack you open at my will and I think it would be a word that would hang on if I ever told it to your contemporaries. "Egg Fitzgerald." How would you like that to go through life with—"Eggie Fitzgerald" or "Bad Egg Fitzgerald" or any form that might occur to fertile minds? Try it once more and I swear to God I will hang it on you and it will be up to you to shake it off. Why borrow trouble?

Love anyhow.

It is very funny to go into a family where the father and mother are devoted to their children. You flatter yourself for an instant that you have secured your friend's ear, for his countenance brightens; then you discover that he has just caught the eye of his babe over your shoulder and is chirruping to him.

RALPH WALDO EMERSON

The fundamental defect of fathers is that they want their children to be a credit to them.

BERTRAND RUSSELL

The Czar's Dinner Service

Patricia Ziegfeld, the daughter of Florenz Ziegfeld and the beautiful actress Billie Burke, confesses in her memoirs she had "an abnormally happy childhood.":

"Dr. Wagner," Daddy said, "one of my oldest and dearest friends, was reduced to eating his dinner tonight from a broken plate. My own coffee cup, I noticed, had a large crack on its rim. No doubt we shall soon be serving our guests out of toothbrush mugs or old Thermos jars."

Mother said she *had* noticed lately that some of the china needed replacing. She said she would see about ordering a few pieces that week.

"No need to bother," Daddy said. "I'll take care of it.". . .

" Have you done anything about ordering that china, Flo?" Mother asked him a few days later. "I'm expecting a large crowd for Sunday dinner."

"It's all taken care of," Daddy assured her. "Don't give it another thought.". . . "Now you run along to New York or you'll be late for your appointment."

As Ernest steered the Rolls out through the iron gates and toward Hastings, Mother, in the back seat, noticed a moving van headed in their direction. She wondered fleetingly who could be moving into the neighborhood. As far as she knew, there wasn't a vacant house for miles. . . .

The dining room table was big enough to seat twenty, but it wasn't big enough to hold the dinner service of the Russian Imperial Court, which was what Daddy had bought to replace Doc Wagner's chipped plate. There was china stacked all over the table and on both sideboards and on each of the twenty dining room chairs and all over the floor. . . .

Mother opened the front door and called, "Hello, I'm home! Where is everybody?" She came down the hall to the dining room. "Did the dishes . . . ?"

Her voice died away. She stood in the doorway, and after a moment she opened her mouth to speak, but nothing emerged except a feeble croak.

She swallowed, moistened her lips, and tried again.

"What is it?" she managed to ask at last in a dry whisper.

"Like it?" Daddy said, beaming. . . .

Mother moved into the room like a sleepwalker. She reached out toward the table and picked up one of the dinner plates and held it in both hands, staring down at it vacantly. . . .

"What—" Mother said hoarsely. She stopped and cleared her throat. "What's this?" she asked.

"Why, that's a dinner plate, Bill," Daddy said. "You know that."

"No," Mother said, still like someone in a trance. "I mean, what's this on the plate?"

"Well, that's sort of a coat of arms," Daddy said. He was beginning to feel vaguely uncomfortable at the way Mother was acting. "A crest. It's on every piece. Solid gold."

"Whose crest?" Mother said, "Whose coat of arms?"

"Former owner," Daddy said, and he rubbed his hands together briskly. "Now! I'll get Sidney down here to clear this stuff out and wash it up and—"

"Who was the former owner?" Mother said.

Daddy glanced at her nervously. . . . There was a brief silence.

"The czar," Daddy said at last. "—Of Russia," he added helpfully.

"How much did you pay for it?" Mother asked.

There was another, and somewhat longer, silence.

"Thirty-eight thousand dollars," Daddy said.

"Ah," Mother said, She put the dinner plate back on the table with infinite care.

"I'll get Sidney right to work," Daddy said in businesslike tones. "He can start stacking it away."

"Where do you suggest stacking it?" Mother said . . . . "In Madison Square Garden?"

Daddy looked around at the cluttered dining room.

"For the first time," Mother said, "I understand exactly what the Russian revolution was all about."

"Well, maybe you're right," Daddy said. "It *does* seem a bit much."

"A bit," Mother said.

"I think I'll have it all returned to the dealer tomorrow," Daddy said.

"A splendid idea," Mother said . . . .

"If you don't mind though," Daddy said, "I think I'll keep one of the dinner plates. Just one."

"Whatever for?" Mother asked.

"For next Sunday," Daddy said. "For Doc Wagner's dinner."

My Father

Many of [my father's] words are still repeated often.

However, his heritage to his children

wasn't words, or possessions,

but an unspoken treasure,

the treasure of his example

as a man and a father.

More than anything I have,

I'm trying to pass that on to my children.

WILL ROGERS, JR.

Gay Bonnets Trimmed With Flowers Negro Metropolitan Opera star Marian Anderson recalls her childhood and the fond feelings she had for her father in her autobiography, My Lord, What a Morning. John Anderson brought much happiness to his family, although he died while he was still a young father:

Life with Mother and Father, while he lived, was a thing of great joy, as I remember it now. It is easy to look back self-indulgently, feeling pleasantly sorry for oneself and saying I didn't have this and I didn't have that. But that is only the grown woman regretting the hardships of a little girl who never thought they were hardships at all. . . .

I remember John Anderson, my father, very clearly. We do not have any photograph of him, but I have a picture in my mind of a man, dark, handsome, tall, and neither too stout nor too thin. I cannot say how tall, but he was well over six feet and stood very erect. Mother is a tiny woman: when she and I stand side by side, her head does not reach quite up to my shoulder. I remember once when she was helping Father put on his tie and she was reaching up on tiptoe. He laughed heartily and told her to get a newspaper to stand on to make herself a little taller.

I don't know all the things my father did to earn a living. As a child I was not concerned. But I know that for many years he was employed by day at the Reading Terminal Market, in the refrigerator room, and we looked forward to his homecoming every evening. At the end of the week—not every week, of course—he would bring home a long, golden bar of pound cake, and my appetite for all other food would vanish. I am told that he sold coal and ice, and he had other jobs. I know he worked hard and looked after his family well. . . .

Easter was [a] big day. Father made it a point to provide us with new bonnets, and he would go to a shop and select them himself. When we were very young he would bring each of us one of the sailor hats then in fashion, with a gay ribbon trailing down the back. Later on he chose different bonnets for each of us, and he always insisted that they be trimmed with flowers. He would wait in the store while a brightly colored bloom was sewed to each hat. When he got home, carrying his gifts in a paper bag, he would take them out happily and present them to us, making sure that they fit.

Father took pride in his work at the Union Baptist Church. He was a special officer there, and among other things had charge of the ushers. He received no pay for his service; it was something that a person did out of love for his religion and duty to his church. He loved his job and never missed a Sunday at church. . . .

As I think it over, I am inclined to say that what I got from my father was idealism. Although he had to live among Yankees, he though of himself as an old-fashioned Southern gentleman, and he lived up to old-fashioned ideals of honor and courtesy. There was something very quixotic about it, but it had a fine flavor of sentiment which I think I imbibed through the skin, as it were.

UPTON SINCLAIR

'An Unspoken Treasure' *Will Rogers, Jr., the son of one of America's all-time favorite humorists, remembers his father with respect and admiration:* "Live in such a way that you would not be ashamed to sell your parrot to the town gossip," my father once said.

If Will Rogers had a rule to live by, maybe that's the one. Anyway, it's the one I remember best.

Many of his words are still repeated often. However, his heritage to his children wasn't words, or possessions, but an unspoken treasure, the treasure of his example as a man and a father. More than anything I have, I'm trying to pass that on to my children.

I remember my father with reverence and laughter. To many he was an Oklahoma cowboy, with a hair lick over his forehead, an infectious grin, twirling a long lariat, and speaking a language of his own that bit big chunks into the sham of his day. He's thought of as a humorist. He was, but he was more, too. He was never an actor, though his name blazed in lights from Hollywood and Broadway to Berlin and Alaska. He was always himself. Even as a wit he was trying to express ideas and ideals, and he would have preferred approval for them rather than applause for his humor.

I do not remember receiving very much lecturing from him at any time. He gave my sister Mary, my brother Jim, and me a good moral tone with the quiet sincerity which was always evident in all he said and did.

When I was a kid I wanted a motor to attach to my bike. I wanted it badly, maybe because none of the other kids had one. But it was very expensive and Father said no.

"But Dad, we're rich." I protested.

Well, the whole roof descended on me. He said no kid of his was ever going to parade any advantage he might have, and I'd better unlearn any such notions at once. Then he muttered something about show-offs, the poor show-off who is always lonely because he's always empty.

That made a big impression on me. Not so much the event, but the meaning my father gave it. Undue emphasis on material things made possessions ends in themselves, and that was morally wrong, if not destructive.

Growing up with that idea can make Christian ethics a habit, though at the time we didn't think of it that way, and my father didn't put it to us that way. The example is always more effective than the sermon. And he often put his ideas to us with a kind of barbed laughter. When any of us felt important or inflated with our knowledge, we had only to remember his remark:

"Everybody is ignorant, only on different subjects.". . .

He was always the example. In those days parents assumed an automatic leadership I don't see in parents today, including myself. My father was the head of the house. He behaved as the head of the house. He was the parent, kindly, generous, but definite. When he said it should be done, it was done. That fashioned us when we were young. . . .

I went to Stanford and majored in philosophy. . . . One day I told my father: "That old Greek, Socrates, put it all in two simple words: 'Know thyself.' "

"Yep, and then get to know the other fellow, too," my father said. "There's always two halves to a whole."

That was pretty good for a cowboy who never got beyond the fourth grade.

He was always suspicious of any one with a pat and absolute answer to every problem. He believed in man's failure as well as his glory, and was willing to accept both, because with his compassion he knew all of us take two steps backwards before we move one step forward.

'Devoted To His Home' *Although blind since nineteen months old, Helen Keller overcame her handicap, achieving world renown both as a writer and a woman of deep spiritual beliefs. Her father's perseverance in finding a proper tutor for his young child was largely responsible for Helen Keller's later success:*

My father was most loving and indulgent, devoted to his home, seldom leaving us, except in the hunting season. He was a great hunter, I have been told, and a celebrated shot. Next to his family he loved his dogs and gun. His hospitality was great, almost to a fault, and he seldom came home without bringing a guest. His special pride was the big garden where, it was said, he raised the finest watermelons and strawberries in the country; and to me he brought the first ripe grapes and the choicest berries. I remember his caressing touch as he led me from tree to tree, from vine to vine, and his eager delight in whatever pleased me.

What you have inherited from your fathers, earn over again for yourselves or it will not be yours.

GOETHE

Lambs and Pugs and Paradise The Winston Churchill whom the world revered was revered also by his daughter, Sarah, but in an exquisitely different way. Her memories of him here lend a new perspective—Churchill the tender father:

I remember an old ram of which he became very fond. He had known it as a lamb and fed it from the bottle. When it grew up it was an absolutely horrible beast and for some extraordinary reason it was called Charmayne. I believe it had been doctored in the hope that it would be less fierce, but things didn't work out that way at all. It used to butt everybody and we children were nervous of the beast. My mother tried to persuade my father to get rid of it, but my father wouldn't. He said: 'How ridiculous, you don't have to be frightened; it is very nice and knows me.'

However, one unfortunate day Charmayne, apparently not realizing the faith my father had placed in him, butted him sharply in the back of the knees, and knocked him flat. Charmayne was never mentioned again and was banished from Paradise! . . .

Mary [Sarah's sister] had a pug. At one point Pug became desperately ill. Mary was in tears, I was in tears. My father was greatly upset at our distress, and although he really thought that poetry, though enjoyable, was a minor sort of thing—he composed this ditty for Mary and me, which went this way and which we all chanted while Puggy was ill:

Oh, what is the matter with poor Puggy-wug?
Pet him and kiss him and give him a hug.
Run and fetch him a suitable drug,
Wrap him up tenderly all in a rug,
That is the way to cure Puggy-wug. . . .

Conversation [at meals] was meant to be general; that did not mean everyone was to speak at once, though of course it frequently resulted in that. We were taught not to mumble—'Say what you have to say, say it clearly or don't say it at all,' were the directions. I found this alarming, and it will test the belief of my friends in later life to learn that I was a silent child. So silent that I became a focal point of teasing—'Sarah hasn't said a thing—come on, Sarah, say something.' There would be a moment of misery and confusion but this was never allowed to go on long. 'Sarah is an oyster, she will not tell us her secrets,' my father would say, and the trend of conversation would pick up again and I would be allowed to sink into my dreams once more. . . .

As I have said, it was important to state clearly and briefly what it was you wished to discuss. Muddle-headedness irritated him, also a stumbling delivery. As I matured I literally would 'tidy my mind' before talking to him seriously. He never failed to appreciate my effort. 'Thank you, my darling, thank you. You have put it very clearly.'

Father (n.): a quarter-master and commissary of subsistence provided by nature for our maintenance in the period before we have learned to live by prey.　　　　　　　　　　　　AMBROSE BIERCE

Father on Stage　*Actress Cornelia Otis Skinner and her father, Otis Skinner, also an actor, first appeared together in a production of Shakespeare's* Richard III. *Here, Miss Skinner recalls her father's initial terror and the subsequent chaos:*

I spoke Anne's opening speech of sorrowing bereavement and Father came forward with Richard's words of insolent accost to which I responded with the second speech of injured outrage. And at that point something happened to Father.

What brought it about I shall never know. Possibly it was an excess of nervousness for me, possibly a blend of emotions at the sudden realization that here, for the first time, he found himself interpreting his favorite playwright with his child, who, being an only one, was perforce also his favorite. Whatever the cause, the result was that when I gave him his next cue, he fixed me with a look of utter blankness and said not a word. . . . I knew it was up to me to say something so what I said was "O wonderful when devils tell the truth!" which being a direct reply to the lines Father had failed to say must have sounded a bit peculiar.

At this, my father suddenly snapped out of his silence and began to speak and what *he* said was even more peculiar. His state of mind changed from one of blankness to one of furious activity, and one in which every line of *Richard III* fled from it and every line of every Shakespearean play he knew, rushed into it. There were bits of *Hamlet*, snatches of *The Merchant*, oddments from *As You Like It* and an occasional sprinkling of *Much Ado*. . . . Every so often he'd pause and when he did, I interpolated my speeches, which, brief as they were, proved to be the only correct ones of the scene to be heard that afternoon. And they too were effective. I spoke them with considerably more hysterical verve than my callow years as an actress would otherwise have permitted, for I was convinced that my father had suddenly gone daft and it was only a strong sense of having to uphold the family name that kept me going along with him. . . . Then I had my final say and exited with shaking knees. . . . The ensuing words he spoke completely correctly, wrapped his cloak about him with a fine swoop and came off to where I was cowering in the wings. . . .

"That was awful," whispered Father.

I could only agree with a whispered uh-huh but added by way of consolation that at least the audience didn't seem to know the difference.

What do I owe to my father? A strong sense of duty and a fearlessness and rigid honesty in the following of convictions.   ROBERT A. MILLIKAN

'Little Nell'   *Elliott Roosevelt, although a physically weak man, was as charming as he was handsome. His personality endeared him to all who knew him, including his daughter, Eleanor Roosevelt, who loved him intensely:*

My father's mother and his brother Theodore's young wife, Alice Lee, died within a few days of each other. The latter left only a little Alice to console the sorrowing young father. My father felt these losses deeply. Very soon, however, in October, 1884, I came into the world, and from all accounts I must have been a more wrinkled and less attractive baby than the average—but to him I was a miracle from Heaven.

I was a shy, solemn child even at the age of two, and I am sure that even when I danced I never smiled. My earliest recollections are of being dressed up and allowed to come down to dance for a group of gentlemen who applauded and laughed as I pirouetted before them. Finally, my father would pick me up and hold me high in the air. He dominated my life as long as he lived, and was the love of my life for many years after he died.

With my father I was perfectly happy. There is still a woodeny painting of a solemn child, a straight bang across her forehead, with an uplifted finger and an admonishing attitude, which he always enjoyed and referred to as "Little Nell scolding Elliott." We had a country house at Hempstead, Long Island, so that he could hunt and play polo. He loved horses and dogs, and we always had both. During this time he was in business, and added to the work and the sports, the gay and popular young couple lived a busy social life. He was the center of my world and all around him loved him. . . .

My father and mother, my little brother and I went to Italy for the winter of 1890 as the first step in the fight for his health and power of self-control.

I remember my father acting as gondolier, taking me out on the Venice canals, singing with the other boatmen, to my intense joy. I loved his voice and, above all, I loved the way he treated me. He called me "Little Nell," after the Little Nell in Dickens' *Old Curiosity Shop*, and I never doubted that I stood first in his heart.

He could, however, be annoyed with me, particularly when I disappointed him in such things as physical courage, and this, unfortunately, I did quite often. We went to Sorrento and I was given a donkey so I could ride over the beautiful roads. One day the others overtook me and offered to let me go with them, but at the first steep descent which they slid down I turned pale, and preferred to stay on the high road. I can remember still the tone of disapproval in my father's voice, though his words of reproof have long since faded away....

Though he was so little with us, my father dominated all this period of my life. Subconsciously I must always have been waiting for his visits. They were irregular, and he rarely sent word before he arrived, but never was I in the house, even in my room two long flights of stairs above the entrance door, that I did not hear his voice the minute he entered the front door. Walking downstairs was far too slow. I slid down the banisters and usually catapulted into his arms before his hat was hung up.

An Ending, A Beginning

Nineteenth-century American poet Emily Dickinson was a recluse who spent her life taking care of her father. Though an invalid, Edward Dickinson was in every other respect the type of the Puritan-descended Yankee. In this selection, Emily Dickinson discovers the beginning of immortality in her father's last day:

The last afternoon that my father lived, though with no premonition, I preferred to be with him, and invented an absence for mother, Vinnie [her sister] being asleep. He seemed peculiarly pleased, as I oftenest stayed with myself; and remarked, as the afternoon withdrew, he "would like it not to end."

His pleasure almost embarrassed me, and my brother coming, I suggested they walk. Next morning I woke him for the train, and saw him no more.

His heart was pure and terrible, and I think no other like it exists.

I am glad there is immortality, but would have tested it myself, before entrusting him. . . .

When I think of my father's lonely life and lonelier death, there is this redress—

> Take all away;
> The only thing worth larceny
> Is left—the immortality.

Forgive Me If I Do   Winston Churchill once requested his daughter Sarah to hold her head high upon his death. In a poem written toward the end of her father's life, she tenderly rejected his advice:

Forgive Me

Forgive me if I do not cry
The day you die,
Streams at some seasons
Wind their way through
   country lanes of beauty
And are dry.

The willow bends its head
To kiss the empty river bed
With the same caress it gave
When in its heyday it was full and high
Oh river know that I remember
The splashing laughing clatter
Of a bubbling day in Spring
When everything was blossoming!

Butterflies still hover
Down the rock bed
And weeds grow strong and
Guard the pebbled way.

In this high noon of nothing
Which is death
Brave flags still wave
Cowslip-parsley, rag weed and sorrel
Shout to me
That Spring is on her way
Comfort, I am still too deaf to hear.

Yet forgive me if I do not cry
The day you die
The simplest reason that I know
You said you'd rather have it so
And that I held my head serenely high
Remembering the love and glory
     that we knew.
Forgive me if I do not cry
The day you die. . .
Forgive me
If I do. . .

Set in Trump Medieval, a Venetian face designed by
Professor Georg Trump of Munich, Germany.
Typography by Grant Dahlstrom,
        set at The Castle Press.
Printed on Hallmark Eggshell Book paper.
        Designed by William Gilmore.